To Joanne,

Thanks for being an ultra ~~li~~ pal. All my love.

Jen

Everlasting Friendship

An Inspired Collection of Writings

ISBN 1-889116-04-1

Printed in the United States of America

First U.S. Edition

Design by
Paragon Communications Group, Inc., Tulsa, Oklahoma

Published by
PENBROOKE PUBLISHING
Tulsa, Oklahoma

Everlasting Friendship

An Inspired Collection of Writings

PENBROOKE
PUBLISHING
Tulsa, Oklahoma

A true friend is
the most precious of all
possessions.

To

Joanne

From

Jen

Date

May 1997

New Friends and Old Friends

Make new friends, but keep the old;
Those are silver, these are gold.
New-made friendships, like new wine,
Age will mellow and refine.
Friendships that have stood the test—
Time and change—are surely best;
Brow may wrinkle, hair grow gray;
Friendship never knows decay.
For 'mid old friends, tried and true,
Once more we our youth renew.
But old friends, alas! may die;
New friends must their place supply.
Cherish friendship in your breast—
New is good, but old is best;
Make new friends, but keep the old;
Those are silver, these are gold.

—Joseph Parry

A Friend in Need Is a Friend Indeed

Two friends were traveling together when a bear suddenly appeared. One of them climbed up a tree in time and remained there hidden. The other, seeing that he would be caught in another moment, lay down on the ground and pretended to be dead. When the bear put its muzzle to him and smelt him all over, he held his breath—for it is said that a bear will not touch a corpse. After it had gone away, the other man came down from the tree and asked his friend what the bear had whispered in his ear. "It told me," he replied, "not to travel in the future with friends who do not stand by one in peril."

—*Aesop*

How sweet, how passing sweet, is solitude!
But grant me still a friend in my retreat,
Whom I may whisper—solitude is sweet.

—*William Cowper*

There Is Always a Place for You

There is always a place for you at my table,
You never need to be invited.
I'll share every crust as long as I'm able,
And know you will be delighted.
There is always a place for you by my fire,
And though it may burn to embers,
If warmth and good cheer are your desire
The friend of your heart remembers!
There is always a place for you by my side,
And should the years tear us apart,
I will face lonely moments more satisfied
With a place for you in my heart!

—Anne Campbell

Friendship needs no words—it is solitude delivered from the anguish of loneliness.

—Dag Hammarskjöld

I keep my friends as misers do their treasure, because, of all the things granted us by wisdom, none is greater or better than friendship.

—Pietro Aretino

A friend may well be reckoned the masterpiece of nature.

—Ralph Waldo Emerson

Friendship

Friendship needs no studied phrases,
Polished face, or winning wiles;
Friendship deals no lavish praises,
Friendship dons no surface smiles.

Friendship follows Nature's diction,
Shuns the blandishments of Art,
Boldly severs truth from fiction,
Speaks the language of the heart.

Friendship favors no condition,
Scorns a narrow-minded creed,

Lovingly fulfills its mission,
Be it word or be it deed.

Friendship cheers the faint and weary,
Makes the timid spirit brave,
Warns the erring, lights the dreary,
Smooths the passage to the grave.

Friendship—pure, unselfish friendship,
All through life's allotted span,
Nurtures, strengthens, widens, lengthens,
Man's relationship with man.

—Anonymous

A Week on the Concord and Merrimack Rivers

No word is oftener on the lips of men than Friendship, and indeed no thought is more familiar to their aspirations. All men are dreaming of it, and its drama, which is always a tragedy, is enacted daily. It is the secret of the universe. You may thread the town, you may wander the country, and none shall ever speak of it, yet thought is everywhere busy about it, and the idea of what is possible in this respect affects our behavior toward all new men and women, and a great many old ones.

—*Henry David Thoreau*

Just Be My Friend

Don't walk in front of me,
I may not follow.
Don't walk behind me,
I may not lead.
Walk beside me,
And just be my friend.

—*Albert Camus*

The greatest thing you'll ever learn is just to love
and be loved in return.

—*Nat King Cole*

What sweetness is left in life, if you take
away friendship? Robbing life of friendship
is like robbing the world of the sun.

—*Cicero*

Acquaintances I would have, but when't depends
not on the number, but the choice of friends.

—*Abraham Cowley*

People share their friendships,
their friendships shape them.

—*Anonymous*

Those friends thou hast, and their adoption tried,
Grapple them unto thy soul with hoops of steel,
But do not dull thy palm with entertainment
Of each new-hatch'd, unfledg'd courage.

—*William Shakespeare*
Hamlet

One friend in a life is much, two are many,
three are hardly possible.

—*Henry Brooks Adams*

A Smile

A smile costs nothing but gives much—
It takes but a moment,
But the memory of it usually lasts forever.
None are so rich that can get along without it—
And none are so poor but that can be made rich by it.
It enriches those who receive
Without making poor those who give—
It creates sunshine in the home,
Fosters good will in business
And is the best antidote for trouble—
And yet it cannot be begged, borrowed or stolen,
For it is of no value.
Unless it is freely given away.

Some people are too busy to give you a smile—
Give them one of yours—
For the good Lord knows
That no one needs a smile so badly
As he or she who has no more smiles left to give.

—*Anonymous*

Plant a seed of friendship;
reap a bouquet of happiness.

—*Lois L. Kaufman*

An Oath of Friendship

I want to be your friend
For ever and ever without break or decay.
When the hills are all flat
And the rivers are all dry,
When it lightens and thunders in winter,
When it rains and snows in summer,
When Heaven and Earth mingle—
Not till then will I part from you.

—From The Book of Songs

A real friend is one who will tell you of your faults
and follies in prosperity, and assist with his
hand and heart in adversity.

—Anonymous

What a thing friendship is, world without end!

—*Robert Browning*

The costliness of keeping friends does not
lie in what one does for them but
in what one, out of consideration for them,
refrains from doing.

—*Henrik Ibsen*

The meeting of two personalities is like the contact of
two chemical substances; if there is any reaction,
both are transformed.

—*Carl Jung*

Nicomachean Ethics

The perfect form of friendship is that between good men who are alike in excellence or virtue. For these friends wish alike for one another's good because they are good men, and they are good *per se.* Those who wish for their friends' good for their friends' sake are friends in the truest sense, since their attitude is determined by what their friends are and not by incidental considerations. Hence their friendship lasts as long as they are good, and goodness or virtue is a thing that lasts.

—*Aristotle*

If You Have a Friend

I you have a friend worth loving,
Love him! Yes, and let him know
That you love him, ere life's evening
Tinge his brow with sunset glow.
Why should good words ne'er be said
Of a friend—till he is dead?

Scatter thus your seeds of kindness
All enriching as you go—
Leave them! Trust the Harvest-Giver;
He will make each seed to grow.
So, until the happy end,
Your life shall never lack a friend.

—*Anonymous*

Since Brass, Nor Stone

Since brass, nor stone, nor earth, nor boundless sea,
But sad mortality o'er-sways their power,
How with this rage shall beauty hold a plea,
Whose action is no stronger than a flower?
O, how shall Summer's honey-breath hold out
Against the wreckful siege of battering days,
When rocks impregnable are not so stout,
Nor gates of steel so strong, but time decays?
O fearful meditation! where, alack,
Shall Time's best jewel from Time's chest lie hid?
Or what strong hand can hold his swift foot back?
Or who his spoil of beauty can forbid?
O, none, unless this miracle have might,
That in black ink my love may still shine bright.

—*William Shakespeare*

The Blessings of Friendship

Old friends are the great blessing of one's latter years. Half a word conveys one's meaning. They have a memory of the same events and have the same mode of thinking. I have young relations that may grow upon me, for my nature is affectionate, but can they grow old friends?

—*Horace Walpole*

A man cannot be said to succeed in life who does not satisfy one friend.

—*Henry David Thoreau*

The only rose without thorns is friendship.

—Madeleine de Scudery

Some friendships are made by nature, some by contract, some by interest, and some by souls.

—Jeremy Taylor

Real friendship is shown in times of trouble; prosperity is full of friends.

—Euripides

A man that hath friends must shew himself friendly: And there is a friend that sticketh closer than a brother.

—Proverbs 18:24

The love of friendship should be gratuitous. You ought not to have or to love a friend for what he will give you. If you love him for the reason that he will supply you with money or some temporal favor, you love the gift rather than him. A friend should be loved freely for himself, and not for anything else.

—*St. Augustine*

Old friends are best: where can you find a new friend who has stood by you as long as the old ones have?

—*Anonymous*

A Wayfaring Song

O who will walk a mile with me
Along life's merry way?
A comrade blithe and full of glee,
Who dares to laugh out loud and free
And let his frolic fancy play,
Like a happy child, through the flowers gay
That fill the field and fringe the way
Where he walks a mile with me.

And who will walk a mile with me
Along life's weary way?

A friend whose heart has eyes to see
The stars shine o'er the darkening lea,
And the quiet rest at the end o' the day—
A friend who knows, and dares to say,
The brave, sweet words that cheer the way
Where he walks a mile with me.

With such a comrade, such a friend,
I fain would walk till journey's end,
Through summer sunshine, winter rain,
And then?—Farewell, we shall meet again!

—*Henry Van Dyke*

'Tis Not in Sunshine Friends Are Made

'Tis not in sunshine friends are made,
But when our skies are gray;
The splendid souls that men possess
Are never on display.
We cannot tell what lies behind
The hasty nod or smile
Or what of worth will come from it
In just a little while.
We only know that when we face
The cares that life must send,
We realize the passer-by
Has changed into a friend.
—*Anonymous*

Each friend represents a world in us, a world possibly not born until they arrive, and it is only by this meeting that a new world is born.

—*Anaïs Nin*

A friend is a person with whom you dare to be yourself.

—*Frank Crane*

The proper office of a friend is to side with you when you are in the wrong. Nearly anyone will side with you when you are in the right.

—*Mark Twain*

The Worth of a Friend

There is one alone, and there is not a second; yea, he hath neither child nor brother: yet is there no end of all his labor; neither is his eye satisfied with riches; neither saith he, For whom do I labour, and bereave my soul of good? This is also vanity, yea, it is a sore travail.

Two are better than one; because they have a good reward for their labour.

For if they fall, the one will lift up his fellow: but woe to him that is alone when he falleth; for he hath not another to help him up.

Again, if two lie together, then they have heat: but how can one be warm alone?

And if one prevail against him, two shall withstand him; and a threefold cord is not quickly broken.

—*Ecclesiastes 4:8-12*

A Week on the Concord and Merrimack Rivers

Friendship takes place between those who have an affinity for one another, and is a perfectly natural and inevitable result. No professions nor advances will avail. . . . The Friend asks no return but that his Friend will religiously accept and wear and not disgrace his apotheosis of him. They cherish each other's hopes. They are kind to each other's dreams. The language of Friendship is not words, but meanings. It is an intelligence above language. One imagines endless conversations with his Friend, in which the tongue shall be loosed, and thoughts be spoken without hesitance or end; but the experience is commonly far otherwise. Acquaintances may come and go, and have a word ready for every occasion; but what puny word shall he utter whose very breath is thought and meaning!

—*Henry David Thoreau*

Friendship is the voluntary discipline
of ignoring faults in one another.

—*Anonymous*

Friendship is a sheltering tree.

—Samuel Taylor Coleridge

How many men, I wonder, does one meet
with, in a lifetime, whom he would choose
for his death-bed companions!

—Nathaniel Hawthorne

True friends, like ivy
and the wall
Both stand together,
and together fall.

—Thomas Carlyle

The Friend Who Just Stands By

When trouble comes your soul to try,
You love the friend who just "stands by."
Perhaps there's nothing he can do—
The thing is strictly up to you;
For there are troubles all your own,
And paths the soul must tread alone;
Time when love cannot smooth the road
Nor friendship lift the heavy load,
But just to know you have a friend
Who will "stand by" until the end,
Whose sympathy through all endures,
Whose warm handclasp is always yours—
It helps, someway, to pull you through,
Although there's nothing he can do.
And so with fervent heart you cry,
"God bless the friend who just stands by!"

—B.Y. Williams

The Meeting

After so long an absence
At last we meet again:
Does the meeting give us pleasure,
Or does it give us pain?

The tree of life has been shaken,
And but few of us linger now,
Like the Prophet's two or three berries
In the top of the uttermost bough.

We cordially greet each other
In the old, familiar tone;
And we think, though we do not say it,
How old and grey he is grown!

We speak of a Merry Christmas
And many a Happy New Year;
But each in his heart is thinking
Of those that are not here.

We speak of friends and their fortunes,
And of what they did and said,
Till the dead alone seem living,
And the living alone seem dead.

And at last we hardly distinguish
Between the ghosts and the guests;
And a mist and shadow of sadness
Steals over our merriest jests.

—Henry Wadsworth Longfellow

Friendship

I really thought you would know yourself to be so certainly entitled to my Friendship, that was a possession, you could to imagine needed any further Deeds or Writings to assure you of it. It is an honest Truth, there's no one living or dead of whom I think oftener, or better than yourself. I look upon You to be, (as to me) in a State between both: you have from me all the passions, & good wishes, that can attend the Living.

—Alexander Pope to Jonathon Swift
August 1723

In friendship there are no gifted or ungifted,
only those who give themselves
and those who withhold themselves.

—*Anonymous*

To throw away an
honest friend is, as it were, to
throw your life away.

—*Sophocles*

Old friends are best.
King James used to call for his old shoes:
they were easiest for his feet.

—*John Selden*

A Discourse on the Nature, Offices, and Measures of Friendship

When all things else are equal, prefer an old friend before a new. If thou meanest to spend thy friend, and make gain of him till he be weary, thou wilt esteem him as a beast of burden, the worse for his age: but if thou esteemest him by noble measures, he will be better to thee by thy being used to him, by trial and experience, by reciprocation of endearments, and a habitual worthiness. An old friend is like old wine, which when a man hath drunk, he doth not desire new, because he saith "the old is better." But every old friend was new once; and if he be worthy, keep the new one till he become old.

—Jeremy Taylor

O friend! O best of friends!
Thy absence more
Than the impending night darkens the
Landscape o'er!

—Henry Wadsworth Longfellow

God Bless You

I seek in prayerful words, dear friend,
My heart's true wish to send you,
That you may know that, far or near,
My loving thoughts attend you.

I cannot find a truer word,
Nor better address you;
Nor song, nor poem have I heard
Is sweeter than God bless you!

God bless you! So I've wished you all
Of brightness life possesses;
For can there any joy at all
Be yours unless God blesses?

God bless you! So I breathe a charm
Lest grief's dark night oppress you,
For how can sorrow bring you harm
If 'tis God's way to bless you?

And so, "through all thy days
May shadows touch thee never—"
But this alone—God bless thee—
Then art thou safe forever.

—Anonymous

However rare true love may be, it is less
so than true friendship.

—La Rochefoucauld

True friendship is like a rose:
we don't realize its beauty until it fades.

—Evelyn Loeb

Life is partly what we make it, and partly what it is
made by the friends whom we choose.

—Tehyi Hsieh

A Little Health, A Little Wealth,
A Little House, and Freedom—
And At The End I'd Like A Friend,
And *Every* Cause To Need Him.

*—Wilfred Owen, postcard to Leslie Gunston
1918*

To Me Fair Friend, You Can Never Be Old

To me, fair friend, you can never be old,
For as you were when first your eye I eyed,
Such seems your beauty still. Three winters cold
Have from the forests shook three summers' pride,
Three beauteous springs to yellow autumn turned
In process of the seasons have I seen,
Three April perfumes in three hot Junes burned,
Since first I saw you fresh, which yet are green.
Ah yet doth beauty, like a dial hand,
Steal from his figure, and no pace perceived;
So your sweet hue, which methinks still doth stand,
Hath motion, and mine eye may be deceived:
For fear of which, hear this, thou age unbred,
Ere you were born was beauty's summer dead.

—*William Shakespeare*

On Friendship

Now friendship is just this and nothing else: complete sympathy in all matters of importance, plus goodwill and affection, and I am inclined to think that with the exception of wisdom, the gods have given nothing finer to men than this. Some people place wealth ahead of it, some good health, some power, some honors, a good many even pleasure. . .the others are unstable things that one can never be sure of, since they depend not upon our own efforts but upon fickle Fortune. Those who say that virtue is man's highest good, are of course very inspiring; but it is to this very virtue that friendship owes its beginning and its identity; without virtue friendship cannot exist at all.

—*Cicero*

Ointment and perfume rejoice the
heart: so doth the sweetness of a man's friend
by hearty counsel.

—*Proverbs 27:9*

A Time To Talk

When a friend calls me from the road
And slows his horse to a meaning walk,
I don't stand still and look around
On all the hills I haven't hoed,
And shout from where I am, What is it?
No, not as there is a time to talk.
I thrust my hoe in the mellow ground,
Blade end up and five feet tall,
And plod: I go up to the stone wall
For a friendly visit.

—Robert Frost

Friendship makes prosperity
more brilliant, and lightens adversity
by dividing and sharing it.

—*Cicero*

A companion loves some agreeable qualities
which a man may possess,
but a friend loves the man himself.

—*James Boswell*

In days that come and days that pass,
let friendship ever last.

—*Anonymous*

Nicomachean Ethics

The very presence of friends is pleasant in both good and bad fortune. Pain is alleviated when friends share sorrow. In this connection, the question might be raised whether friends share a burden, as it were, or whether the truth is rather that the pain is reduced by the pleasantness which their presence brings, and by the thought that they are sharing the sorrow. Let us dismiss the question whether the alleviation is brought about by these or by some other factors. At any rate, it is evident that friendship brings about what we have said it does.

—Aristotle

Home and Friends

The friends that speed in time of need,
When hope's last reed is shaken,
Do show us still that, come what will,
We are not quite forsaken.
Though all were night, if but the light
From friendship's altar crowned us,
'Twould prove the bliss of earth was this:
Our home and friends around us.

—Anonymous

Minutes of Gold

Two or three minutes—two or three hours,
What do they mean in this life of ours?
Not very much if but counted as time,
But minutes of gold and hours sublime,
If only we'll use them once in a while
To make someone happy—make someone smile.
A minute may dry a little lad's tears,
An hour sweep aside trouble of years.
Minutes of my time may bring to an end
Hopelessness somewhere, and bring me a friend.

—Anonymous

Characteristics

In estimating the value of an acquaintance or even a friend, we give a preference to intellectual or convivial over moral qualities. The truth is, that in our habitual intercourse with others, we much oftener require to be amused than assisted. We consider less, therefore, what a person with whom we are intimate is ready to do for us in critical emergencies, than what he has to say on ordinary occasions.

—*William Hazlitt*

They only are true friends who think as one.

—*French Proverb*

Associate yourself with men of good
quality if you esteem your own reputation:
for 'tis better to be alone than in bad company.
—*George Washington*

True friendship speaks with gentle hands
To strengthen one in need,
With loving care and deep concern
As its most special creed.

—*Craig E. Sathoff*

When to the Sessions of Sweet Silent Thought

When to the sessions of sweet silent thought
I summon up remembrance of things past,
I sigh the lack of many a thing I sought,
And with old woes new wail my dear time's waste:
Then can I drown an eye, unused to flow,
For precious friends hid in death's dateless night,
And weep afresh love's long since cancel'd woe,
And moan the expense of many a vanish'd sight:
Then can I grieve at grievances foregone,
And heavily from woe to woe tell o'er
The sad account of fore-bemoaned moan,
Which I new pay as if not paid before.
But the while I think on thee, dear friend,
All losses are restored and sorrows end.

—*William Shakespeare*

Salt of the Earth

New friends I cherish and treasure their worth,
But old friends to me are the salt of the earth.
Friends are like the garments that everyone wears—
New ones are needed for dress-up affairs;
But when we're at leisure, we're more apt to choose
The clothes that we purchased with last season's shoes.

Things we grow used to are the ones we love best—
The ones we are certain have weathered the test.
And isn't it true, since we're talking of friends,
That new ones bring pleasure when everything blends?
But when we want someone who thinks as we do

And who fits, as I said, like last summer's shoe,
We turn to the friends who have stuck through the years,
Who echo our laughter and dry up our tears.
They know every weakness and fault we possess,
But somehow forget them in friendship's caress.

The story is old, yet fragrant and sweet.
I've said it before, but just let me repeat:
New friends I cherish and treasure their worth,
But old friends to me are the salt of the earth.

—*Anonymous*

A Friend's Greeting

I'd like to be the sort of friend that you have been to me;
I'd like to be the help that you've been always glad to be;
I'd like to mean as much to you each minute of the day
As you have meant, old friend, to me along the way.

I'd like to give you back the joy that you have given me,
Yet that were wishing you a need I hope will never be;
I'd like to make you feel as rich as I, who travel on
Undaunted in the darkest hours with you to lean upon.

I'm wishing at this Christmas time that I could but repay
A portion of the gladness that you've strewn along my way;
And could I have one wish this year, this only would it be:
I'd like to be the sort of friend that you have been to me.

—*Edgar A. Guest*

I am not of that feather to shake off my friend
when he must need me.

—William Shakespeare

Friendship is a strong and habitual
inclination in two persons to promote the good
and happiness of one another.

—Eustace Budgell

We shall not cease from exploration and the end of
all our exploring will be to arrive where we started
and know the place for the first time.

—T.S. Eliot

The Influence of a Friend

When such friends are near us we feel that all is well. Perhaps we never saw them before and they may never cross our life's path again; but the influence of their calm, mellow natures is a libation poured upon our discontent, and we feel its healing touch as the ocean feels the mountain stream freshening its brine.

—*Helen Keller*

An old friend can be a garden of true delight.

—*Nick Beilenson*

Then wonder not to see this Soul extend
The bounds, and seek some other self, a Friend:
As swelling Seas to gentle Rivers glide,
To seek repose, and empty out the Tide;
So this full Soul, in narrow limits pent,
Unable to contain her, sought a vent. . . .

—*John Dryden*

Talk not of wasted affection;
Affection never was wasted.

—*Henry Wadsworth Longfellow*

An Hour With Thee

An hour with thee! When earliest day
Dapples with gold the eastern grey,
Oh, what can frame my mind to bear
The toil and turmoil, cark and care,
New griefs, which coming hours unfold,
And sad remembrance of the old?
One hour with thee.

One hour with thee! When burning June
Waves his red flag at pitch of noon;
What shall repay the faithful swain,
His labour on the sultry plain;

And, more than cave or sheltering bough,
Cool feverish blood and throbbing brow?
One hour with thee.

One hour with thee! When sun is set,
Oh, what can teach me to forget
The thankless labours of the day;
The hopes, the wishes, flung away;
The increasing wants, and lessening gains,
The master's pride, who scorns my pains?
One hour with thee.

—*Sir Walter Scott*

Hold a true friend with both your hands.

—*Nigerian Proverb*

Should auld acquaintance be forgot,
And never brought to min'?

—*Robert Burns*

Friendship multiplies the good of life
and divides the evil.
'Tis the sole remedy against misfortune,
the very ventilation of the soul.

—*Baltasar Gracian*

Friends

Not in ourselves does fortune lie,
Nor in the things that gold can buy;
The words of praise that please so well
The lips of other men must tell.
And honor, on which joy depends,
Is but the verdict of our friends.
All happiness that man can know
The friends about him must bestow.

—Anonymous

Do Not Forget Your Cotton Days

Do not forget your cotton days
When robed in cloth of gold;
Among new friends who crowd around
Do not forget the old!

—Anonymous

For he, indeed, who looks into the face of a friend,
beholds, as it were, a copy of himself.

—Cicero

The Excitement of Friendship

Each friend calls out some particular trait in us, and it requires the whole chorus fitly to teach us what we are. This is the imperative need of friendship. A man with few friends is only half-developed; there are whole sides of his nature which are locked up and have never been expressed. He cannot unlock them himself, he cannot even discover them; friends alone can stimulate him and open them.

—Randolph Bourne

My Last Year's Friends Together

Beneath these fruit-tree boughs that shed
Their snow-white blossoms on my head,
With brightest sunshine round me spread
Of spring's unclouded weather
In this sequestered nook how sweet
To sit upon my orchard seat,
And birds and flowers once more to greet,
My last year's friends together.

—*William Wordsworth*

I count myself in nothing else so happy as in
remembering my good friends.

—*William Shakespeare*

True friendship thrives through media
of touch and sight and speech,
but often in the silent times it
most extends its reach.

—*Craig E. Sathoff*

Earth holds no greater good, I think,
Than friendship welded link by link.

—*Edna Jacques*

Friendly Advice

Do not keep the alabaster boxes of your love and tenderness sealed until your friends are dead. Fill their lives with sweetness. Speak approving, cheering words while their ears can hear them and while their hearts can be thrilled by them.

—*Henry Ward Beecher*

The only way to have a friend is
to be one.

—*Ralph Waldo Emerson*

I was angry with my friend;
I told my wrath, my wrath did end.
I was angry with my foe;
I told it not, my wrath did grow.

—*William Blake*

A friend loveth at all times, and a brother is
born for adversity.

—*Proverbs 17:17*

To My Friend

I have never been rich before,
But you have poured
Into my heart's high door
A golden hoard.

My wealth is the vision shared,
The sympathy,
The feast of the soul prepared
By you for me.

Together we wander through
The wooded ways.

Old beauties are green and new
Seen through your gaze.

I look for no greater prize
Than your soft voice.
The steadiness of your eyes
Is my heart's choice.

I have never been rich before,
But I divine
Your step on my sunlit floor
And wealth is mine!

—*Anne Campbell*

Friendship is precious, not only in the shade, but in the sunshine of life; and thanks to a benevolent arrangement of things, the greater part of life is sunshine.

—*Thomas Jefferson*

Friendship is the highest degree of perfection in society.

—*Michel de Montaigne*

We need new friends; some of us are cannibals who have eaten their old friends up; others must have ever-renewed audiences before whom to re-enact the ideal version of their lives.

—*Logan Pearsall Smith*

But Be Contented: When That Fell Arrest

But be contented: when that fell arrest
Without all bail shall carry me away,
My life hath in this line some interest,
Which for memorial still with thee shall stay:
When thou reviewest this, thou dost review
The very part was consecrate to thee.
The earth can have but earth, which is his due;
My spirit is mine, the better part of me:
So then thou hast but lost the dregs of life;
The prey of worms, my body being dead;
The coward conquest of a wretch's knife,
Too base of thee to be remembered.
The worth of that is that which it contains,
And that is this, and this with thee remains.

—*William Shakespeare*

A Legacy

Friend of my many years!
When the great silence falls, at last, on me,
Let me not leave, to pain and sadden thee,
A memory of tears,

But pleasant thoughts alone
Of one who was thy friendship's honored guest
And drank the wine of consolation pressed
From sorrows of thy own.

I leave with thee a sense
Of hands upheld and trials rendered less—
The unselfish joy which is to helpfulness
Its own great recompense

The knowledge that from thine,
As from the garments of the Master, stole
Calmness and strength, virtue which makes whole
And heals without a sign;

Yea more, the assurance strong
That love, which fails of perfect utterance here,
Lives on to fill the heavenly atmosphere
With its immortal song.

—*John Greenleaf Whittier*

I would be friends with you
and have your love.

—*William Shakespeare*

A Discourse on the Nature, Offices, and Measures of Friendship

There are two things which a friend can never pardon, a treacherous blow and the revealing of a secret, because these are against the nature of friendship; they are adulteries of it, and dissolve the union; and in the matters of friendship, which is the marriage of souls, these are the proper causes of divorce: and therefore I shall add this only, that secrecy is the chastity of friendship, and the publication of it is a prostitution and direct debauchery.

—*Jeremy Taylor*

I wonder whether you ever think of the place of friendship in life; what determines it; what it is; what it has of destiny; what it is of design; what of momentary nearness, and passing mood; what of eternity?

—*John Masefield to Audrey Napier-Smith*

Instead of a gem, or even a flower, we should cast the gift of rich thought into the heart of a friend, that would be giving as the angels give.

—*George MacDonald*

The Arrow and the Song

I shot an arrow into the air,
It fell to earth, I knew not where;
For, so swiftly it flew, the sight
Could not follow it in its flight.

I breathed a song into the air,
It fell to earth, I knew not where;
For who has sight so keen and strong,
That it can follow the flight of song?

Long, long afterward, in an oak
I found the arrow, still unbroke;
And the song, from beginning to end,
I found again in the heart of a friend.

—*Henry Wadsworth Longfellow*

Make the attempt if you want to, but you will find that trying to go through life without friendship is like milking a bear to get cream for your morning coffee. It is a whole lot of trouble, and then not worth much after you get it.

—*Zora Neale Hurston*

There is no shop anywhere where one can buy friendship.

—*Antoine de Saint-Exupery*

Friendship

There are two elements that go to the composition of friendship, each so sovereign, that I can detect no superiority in either, no reason why either should be first named. One is Truth. A friend is a person with whom I may be sincere.

The other element of friendship is Tenderness. We are holden to men by every sort of tie, by blood, by pride, by fear, by hope, by lucre, by lust, by hate, by admiration, by every circumstance and badge and trifle, but we can scarce believe that so much character can subsist in another as to draw us by love. Can another be so blessed, and we so pure, that we can offer him tenderness? When a man becomes dear to me, I have touched the goal of fortune.

—*Ralph Waldo Emerson*

One's friends are that part of the human race with which one can be human.

—*Santayana*

The firmest friendships have
been formed in mutual adversity,
as iron is most strongly united
by the fiercest flame.

—Charles Caleb Colton

Letters mingle souls,
thus absent friends speak.

—John Donne

True friendship is a plant of slow growth,
and must undergo and withstand
the shocks of adversity,
before it is entitled to the appellation.

—George Washington

No Friend Like a Sister

For there is no friend like a sister
In calm and stormy weather;
To cheer one on the tedious way,
To fetch one if one goes astray,
To lift one if one totters down,
To strengthen whilst one stands.

—Christina Rossetti

Because of friendship, we see with different eyes not
only our own lives but the entire universe.

—Ignace Lepp

On Friendship

Now friendship possesses many splendid advantages, but of course the finest thing of all about it is that it sends a ray of good hope into the future, and keeps our hearts from faltering or falling by the wayside. For the man who keeps his eye on a true friend, keeps it, so to speak, on a model of himself. For this reason, friends are together when they are separated, they are rich when they are poor, strong when they are weak, and—a thing even harder to explain—they live on after they have died, so great is the honor that follows them, so vivid the memory, so poignant the sorrow.

—*Cicero*

Remember

Remember me when I am gone away,
Gone far away into the silent land;
When you can no more hold me by the hand,
Nor I half turn to go yet turning stay.
Remember me when no more, day by day,
You tell me of our future that you plann'd:
Only remember me; you understand
It will be late to counsel then or pray.
Yet if you should forget me for a while
And afterwards remember, do not grieve:
For if the darkness and corruption leave
A vestige of the thoughts that once I had,
Better by far you should forget and smile
Than that you should remember and be sad.

—*Christina Rossetti*

Friends show their love in times of trouble,
not in happiness.

—*Euripides*

For what do my friends stand?
Not for the clever things they say:
I do not remember them half an
hour after they are spoken.
It is always the unspoken,
the unconscious,
which is their reality to me.

—*Mark Rutherford*

The feeling of friendship is like that of
being comfortably filled with roast beef.

—*Samuel Johnson*

It is so gratifying of you to say in your letter that you like me. Things of that kind, which can be very important, people usually omit to mention. Personally, I have no use for unspoken affections, and so I will most readily reply that I like you a great deal. . . .

—*Sylvia Townsend Warner to Paul Nordoff*

You cannot be friends upon
any other terms than upon the
terms of equality.

—*Woodrow Wilson*

Birds of a Feather

A man who was intending to buy an ass took one on trial and placed it along with his own asses at the manger. It turned its back on all of them save one, the laziest and greediest of the lot; it stood close beside this one and just did nothing. So the man put a halter on it and took it back to its owner, who asked if he thought that was giving it a fair trial. "I don't want any further trial," he answered. "I am quite sure it is like the one that it singled out as a companion."

A man's character is judged by that of the friends whose society he takes pleasure in.

—*Aesop*

My coat and I live comfortably together. It has assumed all my wrinkles, does not hurt me anywhere, has moulded itself on my deformities, and is complacent to all my movements, and I only feel its presence because it keeps me warm. Old coats and old friends are the same thing.

—*Victor Hugo*

The best mirror is an old friend.

—*English Proverb*

Love and Friendship

Love is like the wild rose-briar;
Friendship like the holly tree.
The holly is dark when the rose-briar blooms,
But which will bloom most constantly?

—*Emily Brönte*

What helps us in friendship is not so much the help
our friends actually give as the assurance
we feel concerning that help.

—*Epicurus*

A friend is a rare book,
of which but one copy is made.

—*Anonymous*

Turn my pages,—never mind
If you like not all you find;
Think not all the grains are gold
Sacramento's sand-banks hold. . . .

Best for worst shall make amends,
Find us, keep us, leave us friends
Till, perchance, we meet again,
Benedicite,—Amen!

—*Oliver Wendell Holmes*

Other Penbrooke Books You Will Enjoy:

Love Letters To Remember (ISBN # 1-889116-02-5)
Letters to Mother (ISBN # 1-889116-00-9)
Joy of Christmas (ISBN # 1-889116-09-2)
Sister of Mine (ISBN # 1-889116-08-4)
Significant Acts of Kindness (ISBN # 1-889116-01-7)
The Little Book of Happies (ISBN # 1-889116-03-3)
A Timeless Gift of Love (ISBN # 1-889116-05-X)
My False Teeth Fit Fine, But I Sure Miss My Mind (ISBN # 1-889116-07-6)

To order additional copies of this book, or any of our other books,
call toll-free 1-888-493-2665

P. O. Box 700566
Tulsa, OK 74170